I AM FEBRUARY

By EYE AM

Poetry: I Am February

Copyright © 2019: Eye Am

All rights reserved. No part of this publication may be produced, distributed, or transmitted in any form or by any means, including photocopying, recording, or other electronic or mechanical methods, without the prior written permission of the publisher, except in the case of brief quotations embodied in critical reviews and certain other non-commercial uses permitted by copyright law.

First Printed in United Kingdom 2019

Published by Conscious Dreams Publishing
www.consciousdreamspublishing.com

Illustrated and designed by Drew Sinclair

ISBN: 978-1-912551-50-7

Dedications and Homage

My dedication and homage first and foremost is to the Most High, my mother (RIPP), my children,

My daughter in law,
to the Conscious Dreams Publishing team
for helping to make it possible for the book
I Am February to be here in the physical
manifestation.

Thank you I am eternally grateful for of your contributions

Contents

Etheric

Behind this Smile 10

Communication 12

Happiness 14

Heal 16

Awoke Humanity 18

Thought

Tomorrow.. 22

Food (General) 23

Don't Judge Me 25

Discipline 27

Mice, Cats & Rats 29

Memories... 31

The Father, Son and Holy Ghost 33

Death... 35

Fire

Life on Drugs.. 37

The Narcissist 39

Fire 42

Facebook Lies... 44

Equality 47

The End 49

Water

The Storm 52

Issues Within the Tissues 54

Solo Journey 56

Soul Mate 58

The Motion 60

Air

Time 63

Truly Blessed 65

Mothers 67

Reflection 69

Empaths 71

No Sequel 73

Introduction

I Am February is a book composed straight from my heart inspired by pure love.

I Am February has been composed through my own personal experiences, as well as what I have witnessed through my observations throughout life.

As a poet or an artist, I believe that the best work created, is when we are going through life's experiences. This is when creativity takes on life.

The intent behind the book **I Am February**, is to unlock doors from within, discuss subjects that are often not explored or perceived as taboo. My desire is that February will reach out and touch someone who may be experiencing or has experienced some of what is explored in this book. Some of these experiences can affect every one of us at any given time in our lives. I want this book to remind people that they are not alone. The surety of life is that change is inevitable

My vision is that **I Am February** helps to empower many individuals and brings some kind of comfort, inner peace and clarity.

Nobody deserves to live life unhappy. We all deserve to live our lives to its full potential.

Thank you
I love you
Eye Am

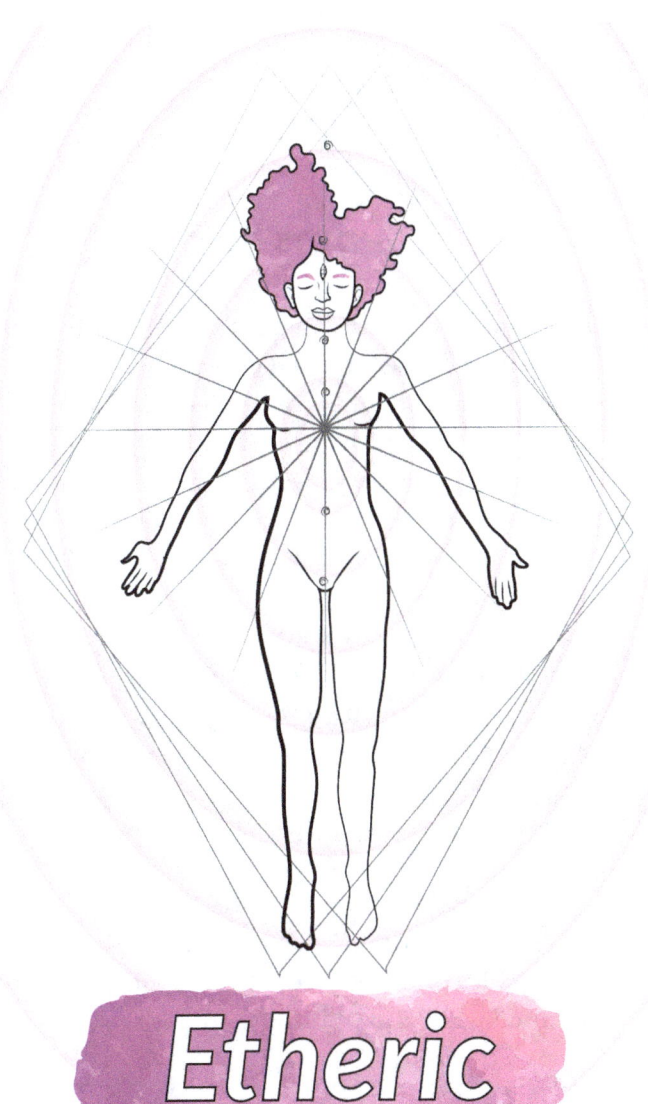

Behind this Smile

Inspiration

You can feel sad but still laugh, be in a crowded room full of people that you know and still feel very alone.

Behind this smile are a thousand stories that will make
you cry if you're human enough inside
Behind this smile, should be bitterness but I have the
strength to replace your hate for me with love, because
love made me and to deny myself of that, makes me as
bad as you, so I use my love to consume you and all the
negative things that you say or do

Behind this smile are stories seen but untold
Stories that would make the most loving
human grow cold
I have surrendered my ego, I have chosen to grow

Behind this smile, is a person like you made of
blood and veins
Someone who bleeds the same
Someone with a heart that can ache
Someone who prays that the suffering inflicted on
mankind by his kind will stop before it's too late

Did you know that you're a reflection of me and I
of you and every time you cause me to grieve you
grieve too?
Believe

Your time will come.
Never spit at the sky
the results are it will fall in your own eye
Today is maybe for me, tomorrow is for you
So think carefully about what you do
because karma will come right back at you
Behind this smile is an innocent man, woman or child
that will no longer allow you to deny the true happiness
that lives inside because the problem is with you not me
but you're too riddled with hate to see.

I continue to smile while I cry behind this smile.

Communication

Inspiration

Sometimes actions speak a lot louder than the words itself or is it how the message is said or received? Do we really understand and listen to what is being communicated?

Whilst deep in conversation I realised I could hear but didn't listen
I was too eager — many would describe me as abrupt
And as someone who always quick to interrupt.

When we converse, we should take time to listen
To avoid broken transmission
Or we will end up missing

Listening as well as talking is an art that's developed as part of our general make up
Some people use braille to communicate instead
There are hundreds of languages and slangs
Some of these signs are used by gangs

So when conversing, listen good because you may miss the important stuff
And if asked to repeat what has been said
The conversation you heard could now be dead

Body language often gives us clues
We can detect if your conversing partner has signs of
the blues,
Body language can show if someone is happy
or maybe sad
You can even detect if little children are withholding
information ... being naughty or bad.

Communication is a lovely thing
we can get across just how were feeling
Whilst communicating, try and throw in an occasional
smile so you look approachable and no information
will be denied

Happiness

Inspiration

Feeling warm and fuzzing inside, knowing everything will be alright. Trust in you and your Higher Self. Most problems have solutions.

Thank you, my Creator, only through you everything is possible.

Happiness is a state of mind
Only changed by you depending on the situation,
experience or time
Being happy with yourself
Not material or wealth
Happiness from a place deep within
On your mind will be constant grin

Knowing no one can break your happiness but you,
loving your life and the things that you do
Staying clear of those who try to steal or oppose.

Be true to self and keep loving you
Even if you feel this, at times, is hard to do
Treat yourself
Recognise this is inner wealth

Be your own lover all the time
Consider others who consider you
For you to love someone else
You have to start with you

Remember you are growing every day
Spread your love and happiness in every way
Happiness is the very start that will open the doors of
desires and opportunities to the heart

Heal

Inspiration

In order for the better of this world, I know that we first need to realise that we are all one. We all need to heal through love, forgiveness, gratitude and understanding, especially of self because we are a reflection of each other.

Every man, woman bleed regardless of race, status, wealth and other material factors that we may sometimes use to us deemed as different from each other.

The whole world needs to heal
and ask for forgiveness whilst we kneel
The things that we inflicted upon each other are bad
Are we human beings really this sad?

The whole world needs to kneel down and pray for
guidance every day on how to drop our wayward
and evil ways

Our lack of love for each other, killings of one
another, sisters hating sisters brothers killing brothers

Bleaching of the skin or going in black face
Regardless of colour we are all one, of the same race
Wealth and material things will keep us separated
and apart
Dig deep inside yourself and follow your heart.

Inside, you will find the true wealth
And this will correct the mental health.

The whole world needs to kneel and heal before it's
too late and break down the barriers of fear, abuse and
mind rape
everything we were taught are all lies
Open your eyes and see the disguise

Stop dishing out hurt, until you have had a taste
It's then you will know real pain
It's then you will realise how futile and sick you were
in this game

Stand still and look in the mirror
Who stares right back at you?
Aren't you human too?
So why hurt someone like you?

Love yourself and others too
When we pour out love it's promotes a
reflection of you
Now is the present, tomorrow may be too late
Because no woman or man knows their fate

The whole world needs to kneel and pray for
forgiveness to heal
Before it's too late
Start your praying and start healing today.

Awoke Humanity

Inspiration

We need to awake from the deep sleep for humanity sake

Humanity is you and humanity me
We are all the same race
Only differences maybe the colour of a man's face

We are made from kindness, we are made from love,
made from creation thus comes all nations

Black, white, yellow or brown
The only way they achieve and succeed to continue with
their greed is to put us down.

They play with us all like a toy
Their ultimate game is confusion and blame
They laugh because some of our actions call for shame
because for some they can't see beyond their game

Regardless of money, status or wealth, they are
not for us
It's all about self
Let's celebrate humanity because it is great
Let's not forget all the bickering and squabbling before
it's too late

Trickery and deceit is their way
They lead the mass to gain their stay
Dumbing people down breeding envy and hate
Separation and divide using idiots as allies
They too are pawns in a game
Eventually they will fall and take some blame

Only man puts a price on another's head and
convinced us all to work hard for our daily bread
When in actual fact we're gonna keep working beyond
70 or until we are dead
The harder we work, the quicker it kills and even when
we are dead our loved ones inherit our bills

Give them back their labels
Let's turn their tables
Give them zero control
Bring out the love from within our souls
Let their plans fail and they will fade away
United we stand, it will block their way.

Forgive your brother, your sister too
Remember they were just as naive as you
Confused and lost in this space and time
Because the true knowledge has been hidden
from mankind

Forget the lies and indoctrination fed through
mainstream education
We now know they're outdated and fabricated
And used to keep us manipulated

Let go of the stories we've been told
that steals our hearts, minds and souls
resulting in our feelings towards each other being cold

Only through dividing of a nation with their
brainwashed education can they control
Free your mind and free your soul
It's a beautiful weapon once you know become awoke
and all secrets will be unfold

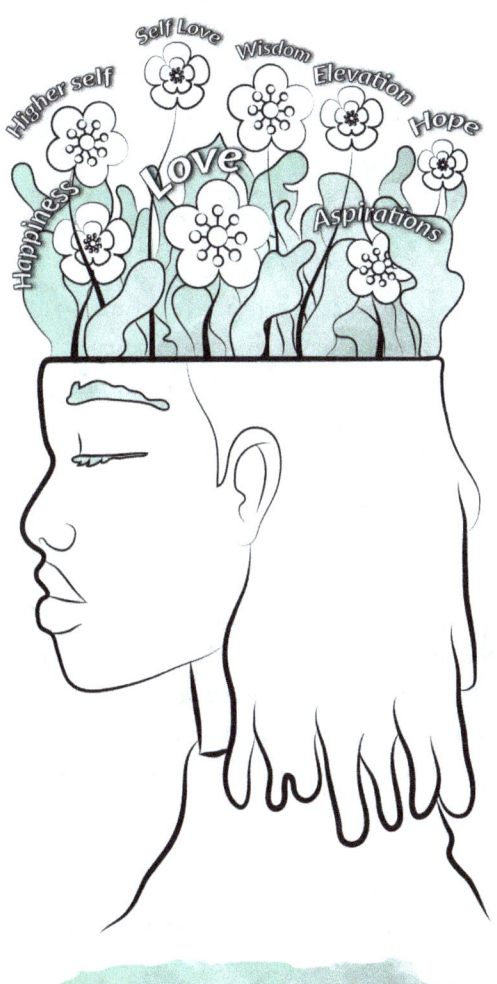

Tomorrow

Inspiration

The past was a dream and the future is promised to no man or woman alive, so embrace the present. It is a gift.

Tomorrow, will it ever come?
But the days, they seem to run
One minute it's seven o'clock
And then it's ten
The next thing you know
It will be April again
The months go so fast so try to live every day as if it is the last
Try to be happy, smile often and laugh
Let go of things that took place in the past
Live for the here and now
Place your focus on how and be grateful for the now and the things that life will bring will be astonishing
I am waiting for tomorrow
To see what it brings
But tomorrow you're so far away
It looks like I will have to settle for today.

Food (General). ®

Inspiration

This poem was created based on my nursing and teaching knowledge. To encourage learning but, at the same time, making learning fun.

Food is fuel, it's an important tool, to keep our bodies functioning great
but we need to adhere to some basic rules before it's too late

Eat healthy every day except the day you fast and pray

Too much of the same thing is never no good
Cook your food and cook it good
Avoid eating rare meat it's full of blood
Bacteria and germs it carries within
And is only really fit for the bin

Eat lots of vegetables and less stodge
Or you will end up like a podge
And if you become a big thing
You will have go to the gym

The gym will keep you healthy through exercise and you may become desirable in someone's eyes

Less sugar in your diet and less salt will stabilise a lot of things
It will keep your heart healthy and it won't sing
Diabetes and heart problems walk hand in hand so choose your food wisely from off the land

Too much salt will send your blood pressure high
This can be scary it happened to I
It will dry you out and give your body drought

Enjoy your food but don't eat too much
Buffet all you can eat will spoil your gut.
Especially if you have it too often and too much

Drink plenty of water every day
This will keep constipation a bay.
Do these things and you will be surprised how eating healthy will open your eyes.

Don't Judge Me

Inspiration

This poem is based on observations such as; how friends sometimes behave, how one can be perceived through their choice of friends. My belief is, be strong-minded and to let no one lead you from your path. Be the leader never the follower.

Don't judge me based on my friends
We may ride together or become strangers, only with time it will be determined and depends
We probably look similar but we are not the same
Our differences are how we play this game

Everyone walks their own way in this life
Some avoid troubles; others live for battles and strife
Some live without direction and may lead a meaningless life
7 brothers with 7 different minds
Some may be bitter, others may be meek and kind
Some may be indecisive, others may have an open mind

Don't judge me based on my friends
We started our lives differently and so shall it be in the end.
Some are now married and are mothers or fathers too
Some travelled the world and now have views with totally different opinions to you

Don't judge me based on my friends
Real friends are loyal to the bitter end
Some friends are liars and devious too
Some are fair-weather, whilst it's sunny and dry but the moment it starts to rain, they say *bye bye*

Some are now strangers we only acknowledge if and when we meet
Different lives we lead,
worlds apart from each other,
No longer seeing each other as a brother

Don't judge me based on my friends
Some are hypocrites, backbiters and I may have kept only one because the others are gone

Discipline

Inspiration

This poem came to me in my younger days in my role as a new parent. There is no handbook to raise children and many have different parenting styles and skills. I have learnt that talking, listening and focusing on your child holistically is far more effective than physical punishment. Physical punishment is detrimental and sends the wrong message.

As I walked into the room
I could sense the tension
Mr Williams had taught his son Jim a lesson
Jim had been extremely bad
He had been tremendously rude
He had been caught truanting school

He had broken one of his father's most important rules
As I stood and stared with starry eyes
I could tell by Jim's expression
That he wanted to cry
I hugged him with love and
I told him *it's alright*
Your father will forgive you and forget
by the end of the night

There's no reason to get upset
Or uptight
Your father was upset with you
Because he feels he is right

As a father, it's his duty
To show love to his son
He has expressed his disappointment with you and now he's done
As you are older and becoming a man
Your father talked firmly with you
Surely you understand?
Your father addressed this issue
Man to man.

Mice, Cats & Rats

Inspiration

Inspired due to the spate of the false flags.

Let's play a game of mice, cats and let's not
forget the rats.
We will keep you busy because you're simple and
incredibly silly
We will divert you from the truth after all you've been
indoctrinated since beyond youth
You know nothing of yourself, your history has been
hidden from you
We've fed you cheese mixed in with lies and meat
To keep you docile and some of you sweet.

We keep a tight watch on our game, we keep you busy to
ensure you lay blame on each other to no avail,
that covers your eyes to keep you from the truth and
believing our lies.

My hand is in your pocket so deep
I work on you whilst you're asleep
I don't have to worry, you will do our job policing each
other and acting like mobs.

You're very simple so we play with your minds
We use distracting tactics things like bling, bling and other silly things to keep you occupied from true meaningful things

This enables us to control and condition mankind. World domination is mine, world domination is what we've almost achieved because the mice, cats and not forgetting the rats help us to continue to reign because you're far too busy playing our game.

Memories

Inspiration

Whilst on duty in the hospital, some many years ago, I listened to an elderly lady who told me a beautiful heartfelt, true story about her life with her late husband, in her younger days. The story brought tears to my eyes and inspired me to compose this poem.

Memories of the past
I thought our lives would always last
My husband died
Now two years have passed

We met in the meadows where the beautiful flowers
grew ever so fast
I remember him telling me that I was a beautiful lass
He put his arms around me
My heart started beating so fast
I'll always remember as I wanted us to never end,
but to last.
He was my husband, my lover, my best friend

This man was mine
Oh, he was so tall, handsome, gentle and so kind.
As we looked at each other we knew there would never
be another

60 blissful years we spent together
Sharing our love, our live and each other
3 children I bear
2 girls, 1 boy we shared
Every day he told me he loved me and showed it
in every way

But now I am left with
Beautiful memories of him and me
As I remembered his face
Before he died
Oh, it looked so grim, he became so thin
If I ever could live my life
All over again
Dear Lord, let it be the same
There is not a moment I would change

Memories of him.

The Father, Son and Holy Ghost

Inspiration

My thoughts shared.

Why is the female represented as a ghost in the bible? Does this contribute to the woman being treated with a lesser value to her equal the male? Isn't the female the gateway to life?

When we pray we say the Father the Son and the
Holy Ghost
Is the female the owner of this post?
A small part for the mother of the child and if in
marriage a punitive part for a wife

A child is from its father's seed and grown inside the
mother's womb
From the womb we all come into the arms of our mum

But yet when we pray we say, the Father, Son and
Holy Ghost
This is not a good representation for any being who
was the host
The female is not a ghost and should be recognised as
the person who bares the most

To bring a life into this world is magical, a present to cherish a near death experience but then through man ignorance they refer to the mum as past tense?
Does this make sense?

To turn this poem upon its head
A ghost is someone who is dead,
When you're dead you become a spirit
Spirituality is what governs mankind
Keeps him straight and makes him divine
Helps him to care and love mankind

From the female's womb we came, to the tomb which we will lay following our days
The day we will die, we will become spirits you and I
Spirits live in the afterlife
This could never be a man's wife

So if the Holy Ghost is the female and the host, the child's first teacher but most importantly imparts her knowledge she does the most.

Death

Inspiration

This poem was written many years ago in my teens when there were more questions than answers. And point remains, there are still more questions than answers. Death is often a taboo subject, should it be?

I wonder why all people die?
It's puzzled me for years
Yet there still is no answer to my fears

When our loved ones die
It leaves remorse, hurt, pain
And bitterness inside
But who's to blame?

For those loved ones
Who are left behind,
Oh, please be strong
For your lives must go on

But what is death?
I still don't know
But I will find out
When it's my turn to go.

Life on Drugs

Inspiration

I have witnessed some people from all walks of life affected by drugs in my community growing up and in my nursing career. This knowledge has enabled me to compose this sad poem.

Doing drugs was not my thing until the day I joined a
bad ring of friends that I thought was cool
I know now I was one hell of a fool.

A few puffs is all it took
Then I became hooked
The worst part is, when I am coming down
My anxiety causes me to feel pain in my body and
all around

I roam the streets for my next fix and when I get it,
I feel sick
Because it has control over me
This terrible entity feeds off my brain
Depleting my chemicals making me go insane

Stealing, mugging, selling things,
This is the life that drugs will bring
Life on drugs is no game
I've hurt many people
And feel no shame

I remember last week
I stole my mother's ring
The one dad bought her before he died
And when she asked me whilst she cried
I looked her straight into her eyes
And told her lies

This habit is wicked, it's horrid, it's cruel
I started cocaine when I was at school
And now I am hooked and a desperate man
I don't even have a life to plan
Don't take drugs to look cool
Because I know now, I was one hell of a fool

The Narcissist

Inspiration

Be careful.

They will charm you to begin with, they lie to gain, the ultimate aim their eyes fixed deeply on your prize

They know their intent and they will be hell bent until they have tasted you and had your scent

They fool you into love with their trickery; soon you will be trapped, entangled in the web and because most women think with their heart and not with their head
And when you know he doesn't love you, he's still captured your heart even then making extremely difficult for you to depart

Their eyes are fixed on your prize, the prize you cover between your thighs
Once they gain and win, watch their smile. It's no more than a grin

When you first meet, the smiles appear so sweet
They will do their utmost best to impress and sweep you off your feet

The conversation flows until your relationship, they
consider, is to be now old
Now their actions become cold.

But for now because they know the goal, they listen
attentively not for interest but to play with you mentally

Twisting your every word making you a liar
Killing your dreams aspirations and desires

Building a negative picture of you, that you don't know
Destroying you slowly taking control
Taking your confidence, tearing it apart
Playing games with your mind and your heart

When you see them for who they really are
You will run a mile, you will run far

With time, strength, courage and confidence you find
and for a while before you leave you will plead,
with yourself
and maybe ask friends for guidance on what to do

Then one day when you're feeling right with you
You will leave all the lies and deceit too
because you will realise that this doesn't benefit you

It brought you to your knees from your feet
It broke you slowly until you were weak

The problem is with him, not with you
Especially when you know that you were true
Don't let this episode define your life
Learn from this episode take my advice

As a small door closes, a better meaningful life poses
Take this opportunity with both hands
Embrace the universe and all of its plans
A better life awaits, so close that finished chapter and don't procrastinate

Fire

Inspiration

Let no one and nothing put your fire out because this fire is infinite it's yours. Own it.

There's a fire inside that will never die
This fire stays alive constantly
This fire has withstood so many things
Especially things heartache can bring
This fire is big and bold like a lion
It's the leader of the pack
The lion that does not fear and will never stand back

This fire within knows his enemies from its friend and when you think this fire has died out, it blazes again
I am sorry my friend

This fire is humble and keen to know, it only works with truth, so watch it grow
Full of wisdom and knowledge this fire is made
The fire is beautiful when ablaze
This fire is far beyond this time or my days.

This fire can love with no end, this fire can love you
but don't try to fool it because it sees through
This fire can capture you and keep you warm or it can
become uncontrollable if place to near a storm

This fire inside stays alive and will grow bigger
and stronger
Only strength it knows, but if you allow tears to
fill my eyes.
Please understand and recognize this fire may burn you
deep inside
Depending on the situation why I cry, if it's through
love, this fire will be calm and remain gentle inside.

No water or other materials can put this fire out
This fire lives deep within me and is a knocker out

This fire will leave this body when it's time to go but
this fire is eternal so nobody knows
There was no beginning so there will be no end
I give thanks for this fire that I lend

Facebook Lies

Inspiration

Abuse comes in many forms. Hurting people hurt people. In a toxic relationship, the abuser will eventually break the victim if the victim does not leave and seek help

We live the Facebook life, the perfect couple you and I
On social media with all the grins and smiles
It's all a fraud, a sham, a big lie.

The life most women would envy me for
My tall, dark, handsome man who I talk of constantly,
who I adore, the man with many problems too deep to
be explored
Silent rivers runs deep that's all I can say
Maybe someone one day some — one else will say
but not me

Every night whilst he sleeps, silent tears I often
weep as I do now, distressed because of the mess this
relationship brings
I never thought the day would come
When I would hear myself repeatedly say *pack up your
things and run, go your way.*

This relationship is over, he's had his fun. It's dead.
To him I am no longer the female that he said was,
the one to share his life and his bed.
Now, metaphorically speaking, I am just another
unnoticed body who helps to warm his bed.

A loveless relationship is where we are at
No communication, no cuddles, no love
No opinions from me because in his words,
I talk pure crap.
This only angers me so I answer back.

Hearing anything from me is like venom. And he is the
person to tame the snake and break its back although
there's no bones to break.
Violence no, it's never been
It's the mental torture that's what is queen

In his words, I am the *negative woman who gets up in his head*,
the woman he tells repeatedly, *I wish you were dead!*
I am the *fool who's evil and cruel and consumed with hate*
The female he has turned his back on and now it's too
late. The one he shuns.
I often wonder am I constant reminder of your mum?

Oh, I can go on but the list is too great. What
happened to us, to you, to me?
I never stopped loving you even though you have
abused me.
Love never dies even if your ego as killed you and I
So, we continue to live our lives in disguise
Facebook lies
It's so fake
But in everyone's eyes, we look so great.

Equality

Inspiration

Equality is only equal on paper. Only he that feels it, knows it. Another individual cannot feel your pain — empathy is good but is not enough.

When I can't do but you can
When I feel uncomfortable in a situation
When I see wrong being played out as right and excuses
are made to justify Alt Right

When I am expected to turn a blind eye
When the glass ceiling is there or the stakes are set high
This becomes frustrating, I won't lie

When I see the world turn on me
Telling me that I am not intelligent enough to be
When our males are rejected and dejected from
corporate life
And only seen as objects of sex and not the man
to marry, to gain a wife, to build a family and a
good make life

When I am not given the respect or the position to be a
leader even when I excel in the role
I'm told *unfortunately ma'am you didn't get the job* and the lame
excuses are told

I apologise for talking Americanized, but I wish you
to follow the poem through my eyes and hopefully
you will understand I feel like a spider caught in your
web of lies

We who know and care are sick of the inequalities and
boundaries you make
the hurdles in our lives, the hearts you break, the
disenfranchise and your lies
If you, too, make excuses to treat someone else as 'less
than', in my eyes you are no different from the rest

The End

Inspiration

Experiences

We had our time
We would sit and talk for hours on end
It's surprising that nothing I said offended you then

I would listen to your stories and you would
listen to mine
So now the honeymoon period is over, no longer
do I shine

Nowadays you may as well be blind
And the words that you speak are so unkind
Anything I say is taken the wrong way and turned
into a fight

The good days are gone, yes, I tried to cling on
through thick and thin knowing deep down,
I would never win
Hoping we could make it rather than break it

I told you when we met that I don't play games,
lay blame nor cheat or lie because this is insane and
certainly not

But here we are so close but yet so far
It's difficult to repair something when it can't be fixed
especially when your heart is no longer in it and my
mind says split

Will I love again? I really don't know
Because what I've learnt about love is it creeps up upon
you so slow
Emotions become bottled up and its becomes
difficult to let go

When the home becomes a house that's grown cold
colder than snow and you can no longer feel your feet
Realise your worth and admit defeat

In time to come when you look back
You will be happier that you are no longer a
part of that
This episode will make you stronger in the end
You will listen to you more carefully when
choosing a friend.

Water

The Storm

Inspiration

Take nothing for granted. Sometimes in our lives we have to lose to gain. Or be destroyed to rebuild. If there is one thing in life that's inevitable, it's change. We need to learn to embrace it all

As my mind races, I see the faces that I feel have neglected me
The ones who turned their back to me or so
I perceived it to be
When there's a storm, it's a rocky time for me but
I'll ride the waves until my mind is free

A rocky journey is ahead of me
I can't see the shore from the sea
All I see is debris and feel the howling of wind that surrounds me

The house that once was me has been broken and destroyed inside of me
And now it floats in the sea drifting along as pieces of wood floating separately

Before the storm came, I knew previously I should have stepped up my game but I didn't because my mind had become dormant and lame

I had made choices at that time to stay in a game that
I knew eventually would try to send me insane
And I know there's no one to blame
I take all responsibility, full claim

But now the storm is here, I realise I have no fear
Wherever it takes me, I fear not because it will not
break me but make a stronger me

So as I search in desperation, in my mind
My negative thoughts are made to decline
I now resign, I know the things that I thought were
mine are only here for a time

As I safely wash up on the shore, my thoughts become
rescued more and more
A sudden calm takes over my being
I realise that I have awoke from a terrible dream

In this life, there will be storms
Even if you feel it's not a norm
Storms that will tear your house into pieces, dissecting
your life almost like a surgeon operating on their
patient with a knife
The moral of this poem is what we do with our life
and how we appreciate the non-materials such as our
husband or wife because everything we cherish and
hold dear in life can be taken away on an unpredicted
stormy day

Issues Within the Tissues

Inspiration

Living in an unhappy or stressful state can lead to disease. Every cell within the body is conscious.

If we are negative, our cells will be negative because we are our cells, therefore we will be more prone to disease.

Let it go, all the negatives got to go
Or it will consume you, didn't you know?
Issues within the tissues,
Not talking about crying
Cheating yourself by lying
But testifying, I am the best, I am in love with me and
chose nothing less,

I am talking about letting go of things that we perceive
as hurt, people we blame for 'causing our pain'
when they can't meet our expectations and of things
we complain
Looking in the mirror instead of acting out as
if insane.
Issues within the tissues kills

Arguments we have over silly things, manipulation,
lies, hating others achievements with green eyes,
smiling with that person you secretly despise

Let it all go and I promise you will see yourself grow
All these things and more will eat your soul clean
from the core
Leaving you with issues within the tissues
Let it all go

Realising life can be beautiful, if we take responsibility
in this game
Remembering every issue can affect each tissue and cell
contributing to making your life easy or making it hell
Thinking positive will keep you well.

Don't get caught up with issues because it will affect
the tissues
Every cell represents your being
Clinging to bitterness and anger will make you unwell
It's like baking cancer within your cells

It's equally important to be aware what you say from
your mouth and meditate in your mind, surround
yourself with peace, pure love and others of like mind
So do not hold on to issues
It will only end up destroying your tissues.
Let it go

Solo Journey

Inspiration

Sometimes in life you may have to go it alone. Solitude is good. It allows time for reflection, self-love, forgiveness, understanding, appreciation and gratitude. You learn to know and love you. Solitude will enable you to grow spiritually. You will become the most important person, especially if you have continuously put others before you.

My solo journey is my own
Sometimes it nice to travel all alone with no-one's bags to carry but my own.

As I travel this meaningful land
I learnt not to trust but to understand
That mankind aren't kind but in fact quite cruel
And only appreciate you if you are their fool
One rule for them, another for you
This kind of game I don't pursue

It's better to run solo than to walk in a pack
The fact is, no one's really got your back
So in layman terms "sack that"

When working solo you have a clearer space not having to deal with difficult people especially those, I classify as a head case

Solo enables you to have time for reflection and time alone
Timing out into your own zone
Building projects
Not listening to others moans or groans
This spiritual journey is mine and mine alone

Sitting back and enjoying the ride
Without an enemy in tow or pretend friend clinging by your side
Hoping that somewhere along you will fail so they can laugh and tell the tale

This solo journey is mine
Simple as it sounds it is divine
No hang ups, no twisted things just dealing with pureness from within and being aware of your surroundings

Growth and spirituality are my goals
To help strengthen and elevate my soul
This is what will keep me bold
To continue to tread this road

Soul Mate

Inspiration

What is meant for you, will be for you. Not even man can change this fact. Man can only delay but not stop. What is meant to be, will.

In this society everything is fast
Even relationships don't last
We are taught indirectly it's okay to have multiple partners along the way
And if we quarrel or disagree we are encouraged again not to make up but to simply flee and told, 'that there are plenty fish in the sea'

When you meet your soul mate, you will no longer date, date and date or chop and change different partners at an alarming rate.
You will know your soul mate right from the start.
Your soul mate will become part of your heart

When you have met your soul mate, you will certainly know because on your faces will be a glow and you both spiritually will grow.
2 that becomes 1 the energy, emotions and bond will be so strong.

Your energies will be entwined like a fine port, or
preserved bottle of wine
You become one in every way
Your friendship will blossom even without any sun rays

Your soul mate will listen to you, your needs and
understand
You will both appreciate each other as you travel the
path of love
hand in hand.

You will build together regardless of all kinds of
weather, elevate each other
And be close to one another like a good mother,
father, sister or brother

People will see you and will know that your relationship
day by day continues to grow because your love for each
other will be so strong your energy speaks volumes and
shows your bond

Your soul mate is a reflection of you
A relationship made almost in heaven it will be
pure and true.
Even a married couple will have nothing on you

If you are lucky during this life time to manifest your
soul mate then you understand this rhyme because
nothing is achieved before its time.
Be patient, wait and bear this in mind
Because when you meet it will be so great

The Motion

Inspiration

We are powerful, but only if we believe in ourselves. Belief can kill or cure. Energy is like fluid... Free. Where attention goes energy flows.

We have free will. Only the body can be imprisoned but not the mind.

The motion of waves in the sea captures as it moves
slowly or fast
It's so free, it resonates deep with the soul, it whispers
whilst it plays out a peaceful story before the eyes
showing and saying you are free
Free to do and free to be whatever you desire just
as the sea

The waves can be deep or calm
Sitting and watching the motion of the sea is beautiful,
refreshing, relaxing and accelerating for me

Strong and powerful is the sea just as the Higher Self
who is the driver who resides within me
Fearless, all love a divine present
Oneness

It all lies within the mind. Eradicate all the fake, the miseducation and start to remake. Rebuke the dormant state, open your eyes and be awake.

Just like the sea you can be free, to do, or to be,
Just like the waves of the sea, we are free
So never be caught up in the illusion and become a slave to your days
Be like the motion of the sea
Be FREE

Time

Inspiration

Time is the most precious commodity. You can replace many things but you can't replace or buy back time. Once it's gone it's gone. So spend your time wisely

There is a time for everything
A time to laugh and a time to grin
A time to recognise you lose to win

A time to express or address without cause for harm or distress
A time when we're feeling unhappy or sad
A time to quit acting like Jack-the-Lad and remember that now you're a man, a dad, a father and fully grown to walk your road but not alone

A time to talk, the time it took to learn to walk, a time to sing, a time to shout
A time to think and be still, this is the time to look deep within, a time to surrender ego a time to connect to the Higher Self, Most High or the Divine

A time to live and remember the now, time is so short so live it wise
And don't get caught up in the disguise

A time to seek help and not be afraid, time when we go to the grave

The beauty of this, is, we are a spiritual beings experiencing it all.
Time is the most precious commodity man has in his hand
So use it wisely whilst in this land
Remain humble even if there's a stumble

Seven times to rise, seven times to fall
Have no regrets, embrace it all
Stand bold and tall.

Remember this and this remember well
Time is a master, man-made, so procreate, do not procrastinate, manifest now, because we are made of greatness, we are great.

Truly Blessed

Inspiration

One day, whilst clearing out my wardrobe, I realised that I had acquired quite a few clothing items and shoes. I realised, for most of us, the more we get the more we want. There are people dying of lack the basics in this world. So I ask myself and I ask you, are you really poor or are you blessed?

The abundance that I have been given are much more than what's been written
That is why I know that I am truly blessed

In the mornings when I awake and open my eyes, I give praise to the Most High because my Creator is worthy and so am I, I know that I am truly blessed

Regardless of what man say, I will continue to give thanks and praise for my days, because the system is all of man's way
The Creator made me perfect in his way so I know that I am truly blessed

When I receive love from many places and from people that look like me and people of different races
I know that I am truly blessed

When there is food on my table and I am able to share, to be kind is to be mankind to show appreciation

compassion, love and care
I know that I am truly blessed

To search through my wardrobe and find many dresses and I know that during this life here on earth, we will encounter some stresses and the mind can play tricks to make you become mentally unfit especially if you let the system get in it
I know our Lord and Saviour can mend and fix
Then I know that I am truly blessed

Trust in the Lord, trust in you.
Never make another dictate to you because it's lies, it's not true
Tell anyone who tries to put you down, in every situation your Creator will be happy to turn things around
We are truly blessed

When you know deep in your heart that the Lord, the Creator is true and your present situation will never determine you
Then you know that you are truly blessed.

The moral of this poem is, stand bold and be strong
Any suffering you may be enduring will soon be gone
And when it's lifted away
You will start to live a brighter day

Stay blessed in spirit and truth in the Most High

Mothers

Inspiration

This is dedicated to my first teacher, the beautiful spiritual being that I was blessed to guide me for the first 37 years of my life.

Mothers are special; they are the gateway to this world
They are much more precious than any diamond, gold, rubies or pearls
A mother's love is pure and kind
The love she has for her children is so divine.

From a baby to adulthood, a mother protects her children ferociously like a lion would her cubs
She's gentle and true and will be the best friend ever for you.

You'll never find love so unconditional and strong
Your mother's love is made with this bond
A love that never fades or faults

So love your mother with all of your heart and look
after her and cherish her before this life departs
Be open, honest and true
So she'll feel appreciated by you.
Life can be mysterious and short.

Tell your mother you love and respect her today and
every day because every day is mother's day whether she
is here or beyond the grave

Reflection

Inspiration

Too often we find faults and judge others, in actual fact, we mirror and attract who we are.

A positive shift of the paradigm will manifest a partner whether for business or for love. However, we first have to work on self. All our answers lie within.

Seek...

I'm dating a man who I find difficult to understand
He is handsome and proud but overly loud
He's materialistic and this makes me feel quite sick
His ideologies are often egotistic
He brags and boasts and talks negative about people the most
He's argumentative, rude and passive aggressive
His lifestyle is way over excessive
He looks down at people that he doesn't even know
and makes comments, passes judgment and makes rude remarks as they go
When he walks past a mirror, he takes a minute to stare at himself
I often wonder whether it is because he as wealth or is he simply full of himself
He works hard to acquire his wealth and most of it is squandered upon himself

He lives in his past and wonders why every relationships
he forms always dies and never lasts
He follows a religion that is more like a cult and
when he's faced with other religions he is rude and
openly blunt
He criticises other religions and promotes his own
His religion is king as he sits on his throne

He often refuses advice, he says, he 'already knows'
If there's two people in this life that will
struggle to grow
It's the ones that are arrogant and the ones who
already know
Water finds its level as many people know
I attracted my reflection and that's simply how it goes
I attracted everything that I represent inside
This man I date is a physical manifestation of my own
mind state
I need to change from within to see the changes
become positive changes to win
Shift your paradigm to attract your worth to attract
your kind
Reflection. Always keep this in mind

Empaths

Inspiration

Empaths especially need to protect their energy as empaths absorb energies quite easily. Empaths are kind, caring individuals who can be quite vulnerable. Especially if the empathetic individual is unaware that he/she is an empath

Stay away from the vampires that roam by day and night
because they will eat your energy
Yes that's right
They'll consume all the good and transfer all their bad
Really?
I ask myself, *are vampires lives this sad?*

They will compete with you
Secretly hate on you for all the things you
represent and do
They could achieve just as you but choose to do
nothing but watch and lose
Empaths, we are their fuel
Stay away for the vampires that roam by day and night
they need your energy, yes, that's right
They stay the same year after year in their lame
dumbed down game
With no desire to make any change
They watch and hate
They keep you close pretending to be your mate and in

their sick mind, against you they debate
We empaths feel and know who you are
We pick up your vibe from near and far
No matter your disguise our energy doesn't lie
They come to eat fruits that they did not sow and as you learn you recognise and know
Keep them far because they are maimed, they are scarred and refuse to take charge for the actions they do...but
NO! They prefer to put their rubbish on you
Empaths be careful, vampires love positive food
They take your good energy and leave you in a mood
They transfer their own and take what they can for themselves and choose to sit around and eat of your wealth
Eating energy that's all they do
When you allow them to get too close to you
They take a dose leaving you drained and they'll be back it's as if it's hunger games
Stay away from the vampires who transfer their own because misery loves company
It hates being alone

No Sequel

Inspiration

This poem was inspired by the sociological relationship between the working class British people and British society itself.

It delves into the thoughts, feelings, ideologies and the experiences of the average working class British male or female while highlighting the struggle of finding identity, security and overcoming everyday obstacles such as money, toxic relationships and the wants to be accepted by society.

It loosely challenges the social norms and the titles that are used to put people into social boxes even if those people do not identify with that particular title.

There is a sleeping power and strength held by such people that will one day be realised.

To conclude, this poem is to tell people they don't have to accept the perceptions of themselves held by society and instead they should challenge such concepts because we are worth more. Humans are more complex and infinite than a word, title, a name, colour or gender.

I'm from broken Britain
Broken dreams is what we're living
Broken homed children growing up without a pot
to piss in
Hoping God listened to the prayers that we
would give him.
Still no religion, never cared that we were sinning.

Working class living, got us wishing that we
were winning
When it's stomach gripping, no food inside the kitchen
Makes you act different, that's when survival
instincts kick in,
forget prison, out here's survival of the fittest.
Still I'm on a mission visions of making multi millions
Now I'm position, prelections to precision given,
Corrupt politicians got me spitting about the system,
Hope my people listen to the rhythm and how I spit it,
Some divisions roll with their Smith & Wesson,
That's for protection to stop their enemies
progression.
We're never threatened, we stay focussed on
the present,
Hope you count your blessings, no one knows when
death is present.
Never been a peasant that's why I'm sovereign with
my message,
used to be aggression now I'm focussed on the essence.
Globalised oppression got my people in depression
that's why we're stressing, sick of being council tenants.
When I'm in a session, I let my passion be reflection of
what I'm stressing
and the things that I'm addressing, many lessons
learned in my adolescence.

Now I'm grown and I'm focussed on profession.
Every step we're getting much better by the second,
Shady 80s legends

Soon to be the one repping, we've got the effort combined with method.
Never let them tell you where you're destined, believe in yourself
Don't let the perception define who you are, you were made with perfection
They're scared of what they don't understand, it's pathetic.
That's why I stand bold for my cause they don't get it,
I spit from the pit of my soul so poetic, repping for broken Britain and everybody in it.
Broken world and broken homes
Loads of hurts and broken hopes
Broken people, woeful groans
Guilty pleasure and painful poems
Spoken English, broken English
Loads of riches broke and English
Sticks and stones may break my bones
But words can hurt when hate is spoken
See no evil, do no evil, hear no evil, speak no evil
Hurting people, hurting people
That's the cycle, there is no sequel
Guilty pleasure and painful poems
Luxury leisure, vagabond, no home
Sticks and stones may break my bones
But words can hurt when hate is spoken
Broken people, keep your head up
And never give up, we've only got us
We've got to be tough
We owe it to us

Although it never feels enough and although you might be going through stuff
When it's all said and done all we got is the love
In this cold world who can you trust? It's like a game of poker, who is the broken never let them bring you down, elevations a must in this cold, cold town.

I put a smile where my frown used to be now
I walk with my head in the clouds feet on the ground get used to me now
It's a new me, unique with the style
I got a whole new outlook, feeling so proud
So if you listen to my sound, play it so loud that your neighbours get pissed off and tell you turn that shit down
Don't let them take your happiness
If you haven't got nothing at least you got that to give
They're scared of what they don't understand,
it's pathetic.
That's why I stand bold for my cause they don't get it,
I spit from the pit of my soul so poetic, repping for broken Britain and everybody in it.

Broken world and broken homes
Loads of hurts and broken hopes
Broken people, woeful groans
Guilty pleasure and painful poems
Spoken English, broken English
Loads of riches broke and English
Sticks and stones may break my bones

But words can hurt when hate is spoken
See no evil, do no evil, hear no evil, speak no evil
Hurting people, hurting people
That's the cycle there is no sequel
Guilty pleasure and painful poems
Luxury leisure, vagabond no home
Stick and stones may break my bones
But words can hurt when hate is spoken
Broke world, fractured by pain
No trust, surrounded by fakes
Heads high

Written by N P Henry

For more information on Eye Am and her poetry visit
www.poetrymakesmotion.com

www.ingramcontent.com/pod-product-compliance
Lightning Source LLC
Chambersburg PA
CBHW071029080526
44587CB00015B/2548